1001 Things Every Teen Should Know Before They Leave Home

(Or Else They'll Come Back)

HARRY H. HARRISON JR.

THOMAS NELSON PUBLISHERS
Since 1798

Table of Contents

Introduction

Every year millions of teens are unleashed into society. And parents are left wondering, "How long will they make it out there?" That's because studies indicate a full 50 percent of them will move back home in five or six years.

And stay for a while.

So it's no wonder that late at night these parents start to worry, "Dear Lord, we didn't cover everything! They could be back by Thursday!"

Then they frantically call their grown children to tell them the million things they don't remember teaching them, but the kids are gaily partying the night away with cell phones turned off in celebration of being liberated from their parents.

Well, all is not lost. The good news is, there are only about a thousand things a teen needs to learn in order to think and act like an adult. And for the most part, it's all here. But remember, the time to start preparing children for adulthood is while they're still young. The alternative is a thirty-year-old teenager losing the remote control, not cleaning their room, and staying out way past their curfew. •

They Should Know Life Is Difficult So They Won't Get Discouraged and Move Home

1. They should know
adulthood is not for sissies.

•

2. They should know they're
graduating into a world where
employers get mad, dishwashers break,
and money is hard to come by.

•

3. They should know
they now pay the bills.

•

4. They should know there will be times
when they can't afford things like beer or
nightclubs. This is no reason to give up.

5. They should know the lifestyle
they enjoyed growing up is not
waiting for them upon graduation.

•

6. They should know a six-figure
salary, a splashy condo, and
a Beamer take time. Or an MBA.

•

7. They should know that just because
things get difficult, it's no reason
to believe God is on vacation.

•

8. They should know their parents
did not prepare them for
every conceivable situation.

9. They should know to persevere
in the face of disappointment.

•

10. They should know everybody isn't
doing better than they are. In fact, most of
the world isn't doing as well as they are.

•

11. They should know that just because
they can't afford a plasma TV or
designer clothing is no reason to
be upset. Their parents probably
can't afford those things either.

•

12. They should know the media
are selling them on a lifestyle that
is essentially unattainable.

13. They should know life isn't fair.
And be grateful for that.

•

14. They should know things are
rarely as good or as bad as they seem.

•

15. They should know the cure for
sitting around feeling miserable
and depressed is to go outside
and find somebody to serve.

•

16. They should know life isn't about
avoiding struggles, but overcoming them.

•

17. They should know that if their
friends' possessions make them feel bad
about themselves, they need new friends.

18. They should know young adulthood means apartments are smaller, clothes are cheaper, money is tighter, and public transportation could be involved.

•

19. They should know the solution to running low on money isn't to start spending more.

•

20. They should know the world is filled with unreasonable people. And they may work for one of them.

•

21. They should know the difference between owning a Mercedes or washing it for a living, is education.

22. They should know "overnight successes" have often toiled twenty years to become one.

•

23. They should know having to pass up partying to work late doesn't mean their life has turned hard.

•

24. They should know to seek the advice of a mentor. Not the wisdom of their unemployed club friends.

•

25. They should know their parents aren't rich. They just have more money now that their kids are out of the house.

26. They should know everybody struggles. Even trust-fund babies.

•

27. They should know that nobody wants to hear them whine.

•

28. They should know everybody has days when the toilets back up. God isn't picking on them.

•

29. They should know that—contrary to popular belief—the amount of money people spend isn't indicative of their wealth, but their values.

30. They should know they've worked all their lives to get to exactly where they are now. Even if they're just sleeping on the couch.

•

31. They should know that just because they're not living the lifestyles of the rich and famous doesn't mean they're a failure. It often means they have a job.

•

32. They should know Bill Gates lost $40 billion in eighteen months, Donald Trump declared bankruptcy, and Michael Jordan couldn't make his high-school basketball team.

33. They should know college and graduate school are hard, time-consuming, and just warm-ups for life.

•

34. They should know if getting a good job were so easy, everybody would have one.

•

35. They should know that if they're trying to keep up with their rich friends, they've lost their priorities.

•

36. They should know people often work years on one business deal just to see it collapse. The successful ones move on.

•

37. They should know successful people don't take rejection personally. They just assume that the other people are wrong.

38. They should know that, when comparing themselves to anyone else, they're comparing God's handiwork.

•

39. They should know overcoming difficult times is how people gain self-respect. And the respect of others.

•

40. They should know that self-discipline is a key to solving life's problems.

•

41. They should know to not lose their belief in miracles.

•

42. They should know the secret to solving paralyzing problems isn't to take to the couch, but to start taking action.

43. They should know life's challenges
make us stronger, better, healthier,
more spiritual, and more grateful
human beings. After we freak out.

•

44. They should know the fear
of pain can make people goofy.

•

45. They should know that in five years
they don't have to be the same person
they are today. They could have earned
a law degree, fed the hungry in Africa,
or defended their country.

•

46. They should know victims
are never happy.

47. They should know life is
all about negotiation. A skill
they learned when they were six.

•

48. They should know to not wait
until there are helicopters circling
overhead to start a prayer life.

•

49. They should know that if they get
laid off, it doesn't mean they'll spend
the rest of their life in a Chevrolet.
It just means God has other plans.

•

50. They should know the biggest difference between childhood and adulthood is
that in adulthood you really can't give up.

51. They should know they'll feel a lot better about everything if they get a good night's sleep. Exhaustion can make everything seem darker.

•

52. They should know that if they make one person's life easier today, God will be pleased with their efforts. Start with their mom.

•

53. They should know that taking on debt for student loans is often the only path to a professional career.

•

54. They should know growing up takes moving out. And moving on.

They Should Know How to Not Look Stupid Because People Will Notice and They'll Have to Move Home

55. They should know truly independent people don't scream they're independent with their hand held out.

•

56. They should know how to type without looking at the keyboard. Or be prepared for a minimum-wage job with hazardous duty pay.

•

57. They should know to show up on time. For interviews. For class. For work. For relationships. Showing up late says they're goobers.

•

58. They should know many companies would prefer not to see their tattoos. Or nose ring.

59. They need to know their role models shouldn't be one another.

•

60. They should know that just because they don't know what a person is talking about doesn't mean that person actually knows what he's talking about. He could be a loon with charts.

•

61. They should know Hollywood isn't hiring.

•

62. They should know to leave their Social Security card at home. Hidden.

•

63. They should know the successful person does things other people don't like to do. Like get organized.

64. They should know that if they
sleep around, it will get around.

•

65. They should know to stop complain-
ing. Ninety percent of the people
who hear it don't care, and the other
10 percent are happy they're miserable.

•

66. They should know to keep up
with what's going on in the world.

•

67. They should know that they can now
be personally sued for their stupid actions.

•

68. They should know how to
complete a sentence without using
the words "like," "you know,
"awesome," and "Oh my God."

69. They should know that people with a weak, flabby handshake make others wonder about their spine.

•

70. They should know to show up for work clear-eyed and alert. Not exhausted, hung over, and begging people for aspirin.

•

71. They should know "$30,000-a-year millionaires" aren't fooling anybody but themselves.

•

72. They should know the way they dress at eight p.m. can make them look irresponsible at eight a.m.

73. They should know hanging out with heavy drinkers, drug users, and partyers, is a surefire way to start thinking like a heavy drinker, drug user, and partyer.

•

74. They should know that talking like a rapper will scare people.

•

75. They should consider that yes, as impossible as it may seem, they could be wrong.

•

76. They should know one of the best tools for not looking dumb is to ask questions of people.

77. They should know it's impossible
to learn anything while talking.

•

78. They should know to refrain from
sending any e-mail written in the heat
of the moment. In certain circum-
stances, it could be called evidence.

•

79. They should know to not
naively believe everyone is good
and has their best interest at heart.

•

80. They should know to never believe
e-mails saying they just won a contest
in Belgium they never entered.

81. They should know standing in a strange part of town at 9 p.m. looking lost and confused invites trouble.

•

82. They should know the quickest way to get rid of a crowd of people is to start talking about themselves.

•

83. They should know to not announce they're seeking answers from a tarot card reader. People will assume they're part of the lunatic fringe.

•

84. They should know how to read fast and well. This helps with applications, instructions, and contracts.

•

85. They should know how to listen without tuning out 50 percent of what is said.

•

86. They should know that graduating from college without having earned any money makes people wonder if they're terminally lazy.

•

87. They should know spell-check can help them look smarter. Careers are derailed over poor writing and spelling.

•

88. They should know "Whatever" isn't a sentence. It's evidence of a fragile mind.

•

89. They should know that if they don't know what they're talking about, stay silent.

90. They should know to not believe everything they hear.

•

91. They should know that one of the signs of a loser is to never plan ahead. Going with the flow usually means going down the drain.

•

92. They should know a successful college or grad student studies sitting up (not lying down), at a desk (not in bed), with the lights on (not off), and for extended periods of time (not during commercials).

93. They should know the differences between the governments of the United States and China. Voting, for starters.

•

94. They should know that boasting makes people wonder what's really wrong with them.

•

95. They should know how to carry a conversation without using profanity.

•

96. They should know to follow instructions. Houses are set on fire over this.

97. They should know what government agency is in charge of what. If they call city hall about their income tax return, they'll be hung up on.

•

98. They should know the meaning of words before confidently using them in conversation.

•

99. They should know to avoid the emission of deadly bodily odors. People would rather stand next to an attack dog.

•

100. They should know the names of our enemies, i.e., Bin Laden, Chavez, Hussein, Al-Zawahiri, and Kim Jong-Il.

101. They should know enough math skills to determine if they can pass up the next gas station.

•

102. They should know to not mumble. Twenty-year-olds may understand each other, but nobody else does.

•

103. They should know how to defend a position without yelling, swearing, or door slamming. And it's a bonus if they know what they're talking about.

•

104. They should know alcohol causes bad breath. They should also know that while they can't smell it, everybody else can.

105. They should know to write notes
to themselves. The alternative is
to rely on a memory that can't
remember to call their mother.

•

106. They should know telling the
truth drastically limits one's chances
of being humiliated, fired, or sued.

•

107. They should know good manners
stun people so, that favors, promotions,
and recommendations follow.

•

108. They should know that if they
listen more than they talk, they will curiously be known as a good conversationalist.

109. They should know that having three or four drinks doesn't make one sound any smarter. Unless they're talking to a person who's had five.

•

110. They should know to not use a credit card in a restaurant or club if they haven't paid the bill in a few months. Their companions will be hugely unimpressed when it's rejected.

•

111. They should know the fine art of small talk. It beats standing alone with a potted plant all night when they could be chatting with the most important person in the room.

112. They should know what the
Berlin Wall was, what it symbolized,
what happened to it, and that
it was in Berlin. Germany.

•

113. They should know to read the
Bible before they argue about it.

•

114. They should know to not confuse
fiction with nonfiction books and
movies. It's the latest rage today.

•

115. They should know what Marxism
is. And why a Marxist candidate for
even a dogcatcher isn't a good idea.

•

They Should Know How to Get a Job So They Can Make Their Own Money and Not Have to Move Home

116. They should know what they're
capable of doing for a living.
Not just what they'd like to do.

•

117. They should know the best time
to start networking is way before they
actually need a network. Or else they're
just hitting up strangers for jobs.

•

118. They should know to walk into
the college career center the day
they walk into college. This way
they have four years to prepare
for the right job. Not four weeks.

119. They should know the alternative to spending four years on internships, major-related jobs, volunteer work, student organizations, professional associations, and networking is often bartending. Despite dropping $80,000 on an education.

•

120. They should know to ditch their high-school student attitudes and behaviors. Time for adult thinking.

•

121. They should know to find a job they'd be comfortable taking their mother to.

122. They should know employers care more about a college degree than where the diploma is from. Most CEOs of the biggest corporations didn't go to prestigious schools.

•

123. They should know their chances of becoming among the biggest earners in any profession—like acting—are extremely small.

•

124. They should know summer internships lead to job offers.

•

125. They should know that finding a job is, in itself, a full-time job. With weekend and evening work involved.

126. They should know their resumé has fifteen seconds to get the attention of an HR director.

•

127. They should know that if they wait until they graduate from college to pump up their resumé, they've waited too long.

•

128. They should know building a resumé doesn't mean lying or exaggerating. It means accomplishing.

•

129. They should know to create their resumé in four formats: a print version, a scannable version, a plaintext version, and an e-mail version. Same resumé, four formats.

130. They should know the print version of their resumé is where to use bullets, italics, and of course, spell-check.

•

131. They should know to use the plaintext version (same info but without italics or bullets) to paste into online forms or databases.

•

132. They should know to always send their resumé in the body of an e-mail, not just as an attachment.

•

133. They should know that, while posting their resumé is mandatory, most jobs come from personal contacts like their parents or their parents' boring friends.

134. They should know to Google
their name. See what pops up.
Prospective employers will.

•

135. They should know their cover
letter is the door opener. Or door closer.

•

136. They should know that their
cover letter should stress their education,
their experience, their professionalism,
and the opportunity they are seeking.
Not their family's connections.

•

137. They should know to be careful
with the information they put on
personal Web sites. Employers don't
need to know about race, religion, health
problems, or people they like to date.

138. They should know there is
a plethora of books, software,
and services to help them create
a résumé and a cover letter.
And their competition is using them.

•

139. They should know what their
references plan to say. If they plan
to say, "She can drink shooters
all night long without getting
silly-faced," get another reference.

•

140. They should know to never start a
cover letter with "Dear Sir or Madam."
It says they were too unmotivated to
learn the interviewer's name.

141. They should know to apply for a specific position. Saying, "I'll do anything" on their résumé will cause it to mysteriously disappear.

•

142. They should know the salary range before they go in for the interview. The Internet, friends, and other employees help here.

•

143. They should know speaking a foreign language will increase their job chances exponentially. Speaking Japanese or Mandarin will get them a nice hiring bonus.

144. They should know the people they meet in college and graduate schools are future clients, customers, or employers. Don't lose track of them.

•

145. They should know they might have to go to specific cities to find a job in certain industries. For instance, the fashion industry in Billings, Montana, isn't huge.

•

146. They should know employers will be checking their MySpace or Facebook pages. What their friends find hilarious will usually result in rejection letters.

147. They should know that handing out résumés at medical centers to anyone who even looks like a pharmaceutical salesperson is the initiative it takes to land those kinds of hard-to-find jobs.

•

148. They should know to avoid résumé inflation. Claiming unearned honors, achievements, and skills will only make them look ridiculous.

•

149. They should know the difference between networking and hanging in bars late at night with a bunch of out-of-work goobers talking about getting a job.

150. They should know to hand out, mail, or personally deliver fifty résumés a day. Or else spend their days moaning about how they don't have a job.

•

151. They should know all interviewers will ask, "So, what do you know about us?" If they respond with a blank stare, they'll be home before lunch.

•

152. They should know to never, ever bad-mouth another company or person in an interview. Kiss of death.

•

153. They should know to not freak out if they're given a personality test. It takes all kinds of people to make up a company.

154. They should realize the issue
of their grade point average will come
up. Something to think about
while blowing off a test.

•

155. They should know sweaty armpits,
cursing, and erratic driving are the result
of waiting until the day of the interview
to drive to its location for the first time.

•

156. They should know to arrive early
to each interview if for no other
reason than to avoid a speeding ticket.

•

157. They should know to not
dress like a model or rock star unless
they're interviewing to be one.

158. They should know to ask God to walk into the interview with them.

•

159. They should know to collect their thoughts before answering any question. Rambling will only serve to make them look mental.

•

THEY SHOULD KNOW TO PLAN AND PRACTICE THEIR ANSWERS TO THE FOLLOWING QUESTIONS:

160. *"Tell me about yourself."* They need to be able to get to the point about their goals, experience, interests, and communication skills.

161. *"What are your strengths?"* This is the key time to point out their characteristics that make them perfect for the job.

•

162. *"What are your weaknesses?"* They should know that saying, "I work too hard" or "I'm a perfectionist" makes inter-viewers gag. Just point out their obvious inexperience as the greatest weakness.

•

163. *"Why do you want to work here?"* This is where Internet research pays off. They should say, "I've always wanted to work for a company that does things the way you do..." and talk about what they've learned.

164. *"Why should we hire you?"*
This is a good time to mention the
word *desire* as well as talk about
their unique strengths and experiences
that make them ideal for the job.

•

165. *"What would you do in a particular
situation?"* This is a trick question.
They should ask the interviewer,
"What's my goal?" before responding.

•

166. They should remember the purpose
of the first interview: to get a second one.

167. They should know to ask how their performance will be measured, will they be transferred, and how top employees are rewarded.

•

168. They should know to ask questions other prospects might not: "Is management stable? What about training programs? Will the company fund additional education?"

•

169. They should know to not give out salary information until they receive an offer. And this could take two or three interviews.

170. They should know a thank-you note will make them look more professional than the last ten goobers who walked in the door, and they can add anything they forgot to say.

•

171. They should know that every interview is a networking opportunity. Their interviewer knows somebody who knows somebody.

•

172. They should know second and third interviews often happen out of town, meaning they have to be even more buttoned up and organized.

173. They should know most starting salaries are barely enough to live on, no matter what it looks like on TV.

•

174. They should know to ask if the company is going to move them to an expensive part of the country and if the salary takes that into question. The salary might go a little higher. (They can research standards of living and crime rates online and come up with their own figure to negotiate.)

175. They should know to interview with the person who will be their actual boss. This prevents any surprises down the road.

•

176. They should know to ask what happened to the person who had the job before them. Were there promoted? Fired? Transferred? Eloped with the boss? They need to know.

•

177. They should know to remember the goal in negotiations is not to get fifty grand a year. It's to get hired, get trained, get experience, build their value, get money, and get out of the house.

178. They should know it's likely they'll have to pass a urine test before employers sign on the dotted line.

•

179. They should know to not hold out for the "perfect" job. They have forty or fifty years to find that.

•

180. They should know to not over negotiate once they've gotten a fair offer.

•

181. They should know to celebrate their job offer. It's a very cool thing.

182. They should know to take
the health insurance offered even
though it reduces their paycheck.
A ten-thousand-dollar-a-day hospital-
ization will really ruin party plans.

•

183. They should know to sign up for
their company's Medical Flex Account.
It's a great way to pay for eyeglasses,
LASIK surgery, and dental
procedures with pre-tax money.

•

184. They should know to never
forget who their Employer really is.

They Should Know How to Keep a Job and Get Promoted So They Don't Get Fired and Have to Move Home

185. They should know that beginning right now they're in an intense, high-stakes competition for a life unimaginable by most of the planet.

•

186. They should realize that college didn't teach them half the stuff they need to know about their job.

•

187. They should know that a business meeting interrupted by a cell phone ringtone of "Let's Get Drunk" will not be deemed a success.

•

188. They should know to think long term. Success doesn't happen overnight. It often takes years.

189. They should know how to do two or three things at once. In the business world, it's called multi-tasking.

•

190. They should know proper grammar. One day they will have to write a business letter or make a presentation, and they don't want to sound like a complete tater.

•

191. They should know going to work drunk or high, while currently fashionable on TV, will get them canned.

•

192. They should know to be more concerned with showing up on time than taking time off.

193. They should be dependable.
Show-up-on-time dependable,
get-work-done-on time dependable,
stay-late-if-you-need-me-to dependable.

•

194. They should know to
raise their hand when they're
confused or sinking under water.
Don't wait till the exit interview.

•

195. They should know the keys
to promotion are ambition, creativity,
and the ability to grow on the job.

•

196. They should know the world
beyond their friends cares little that
they have a Rolex or Mercedes.
The world cares about results.

65

197. They should know that if they don't spread office gossip, they'll never have to apologize to anybody.

•

198. They should know to prepare for meetings and presentations. The alternatives are hot flashes, hiccups, and looking stupid.

•

199. They should know to always let the boss know what they're doing. Don't assume bosses know.

•

200. They should know co-workers who don't like them can derail career plans. Think teamwork.

201. They should know to never use the words *not my job* if they're making long-term career plans.

•

202. They should know one key to success is to keep a journal of their accomplishments and points to improve on. The trick is to refer to it weekly.

•

203. They should know to congratulate their co-workers for jobs well done. Even if they hate their guts and feel like management likes them better.

•

204. They should know the first year on the job impacts their long-term advancement, salary, satisfaction, and career track.

205. They should know nobody likes ideas from people who don't know what they're talking about. Especially newly hired graduates who think they know everything.

•

206. They should know a business lunch is no different than any other business meeting except you have the opportunity to ruin your clothes. Order accordingly.

•

207. They should know the only people allowed to be prima are the bosses and the people who bring in the most business.

208. They should know to stay alert in meetings. Yawning and napping should have ended in English lit.

•

209. They should understand that every business, even a dentist office, is about politics.

•

210. They should know to say "thank you" to co-workers regularly. It breeds enormous goodwill.

•

211. They should know to learn the janitor's name.

212. They should know that taking office supplies, making personal long-distance calls on the company phone, and padding expenses is stealing.

•

213. They should know to read the company manual.

•

214. They should know to not criticize anything the first six months. They could be stomping on the president's idea and not realize it.

•

215. They should know showing up for work exhausted and hung over is only okay as long as everybody went to the same party.

216. They should know to take a twenty-minute power nap at noon if they need one. And where.

•

217. They should know it's perfectly okay to suck up to the boss.

•

218. They should know that not everything they do will generate praise. Even if it's well done.

•

219. They should know jerks sometimes have a way of getting promoted. It happens.

220. They should know to bring their boss a solution every time they bring up a problem.

•

221. They should know how to figure things out on their own. Most of the world's secrets can be unlocked with Google, determination, and coffee.

•

222. They should know excuses don't lead to promotions.

•

223. They should know helping out fellow employees is a proven way to build goodwill.

224. They should know if everyone
at the office is wearing blue suits,
they need to wear a blue suit.

•

225. They should know that
making themselves irreplaceable
to their clients and bosses is a
secret to raises and promotions.

•

226. They should know to volunteer
for challenging assignments
It's how to get noticed.

•

227. They should know how to do
a presentation with something more
interesting than PowerPoint.

228. They should know the office is no place to look like they're working for Vogue. Unless, of course, they work for Vogue.

•

229. They should know that if they dress provocatively on the job, everyone will notice: clients, bosses, bosses' wives. Human Resources.

•

230. They should know they have a choice: partying all night or functioning effectively in the business world the next morning.

•

231. They should know how to discern unspoken, on-the-job expectations.

232. They should realize success in any job is about beating the competition. And the competition is often well educated, well connected, and in the next office.

•

233. They should know that whining about not being promoted will get them labeled a malcontent.

•

234. They should know to find a mentor at the office who can champion their cause. This is how careers are launched.

•

235. They should know to ask for more responsibility before they ask for a raise.

236. They should know to be ready to move. Some promotions are fifteen hundred miles away.

•

237. They should know that no one gets promoted six months into a job. But a lot of people get promoted because the person above them impatiently quits.

•

238. They should know to keep their thoughts about the company they work for to themselves. And off the Internet.

•

239. They should know they'll get more notice for working late than they will for coming in early.

240. They should know the power of handwritten notes. It's a tool of future CEOs.

•

241. They should know that if they don't set goals, they'll wake up in Duluth one morning wondering what happened to their career.

•

242. They should know long, boring, tedious preparation is the key to the Ferrari.

•

243. They should know to become immune to failure. It didn't bother them in junior high.

244. They should know it often takes longer than eight-to-five to get the job done.

•

245. They should know it's poisonous to compare salaries with anyone else in the office.

•

246. They should know successful people are delusional: they're not as good or as smart or as necessary as they think they are. But their confidence takes them to the top.

•

247. They should know to make a list every night of what they need to accomplish the next day. Knowing what to do is how things get done.

248. They should know to be careful
with office romances. And more
careful with office romance breakups.

•

249. They should know that
instead of buying their boss a
Christmas gift, make a charitable
donation in their name instead.

•

250. They should know to take
all the vacation days they're due.
Their coworkers are tired of them too.

•

251. They should know that if they
do their job well, they are entitled
to raises and promotions. And often
these have to be negotiated.

252. They should know that
to effectively negotiate they must
have a clear goal in mind, be patient,
be quietly stubborn, and recognize
when a good deal is on the table.

•

253. They need to know there's
nothing disloyal about interviewing
with other companies. It's how
people get raises faster.

•

254. They should know to not criticize
their current situation when interviewing. They'll just come off as a moaner.

255. They should know a great
negotiation ploy in discussing raises
is talking about another job offer. It's
even more effective if they have one.

•

256. They should know to, rather
confront their boss about a raise, enlist
their boss's help in getting one.

•

257. They should know that if they've
done their work well but others are getting
raises and promotions, it's time to go.

258. They should know to take several
things into consideration besides
money when deciding on another job.
Like opportunity, benefits, and travel.

•

259. They should know to not
be afraid of changing jobs.
Be afraid of losing their passion.

•

260. They should know to not resign
until they've accepted another offer
in writing. Until then, it's all rumor.

261. They should know to resign the right way: personally, to their boss, and without bad-mouthing anybody.

•

262. They should know one of life's most baffling mysteries is how people come in and out of one's life. Don't burn any bridges.

•

263. They should know to send their resumé to 6figurejobs.com. Hey, miracles happen.

•

264. They should remember the first job is just that.

They Should Know How to Live On a Starting Salary So They Won't Go Broke and Have to Move Home

265. They should know that life, unlike college, doesn't come with a meal card. Budgeting is in order.

•

266. They should know they can save a fortune by cooking. Their kitchen isn't there to just store beer.

•

267. They should know all that's required to save $10 to $20 on a meal is a pan, a can opener, a spatula, and an old fridge.

268. They should remember the cost of partying is sky-high: ten dollars for admissions, fifteen dollars for drinks, plus cab fare, parking fees, a tip for the doorman...It's easy to spend a week's salary in one night.

•

269. They should know they can live on what they make. They just can't live like they want to on what they make.

•

270. They should know to pay off their fines and rejoin the library. It's a way to save a fortune in book and movie rental costs.

271. They should know public transportation is cheaper than expensive gasoline and parking meters.

•

272. They should know the prices in supermarkets are two to three times less than in convenience stores. Of course, it may require shopping at an hour other than 3:00 a.m.

•

273. They should know the "free" gifts that credit cards and banks offer never justify the rates. If they need a toaster, go buy one.

274. They should know the first kind of clothing to invest in should be well-made business clothes. Partying clothes are only important if they work in a nightclub.

•

275. They should know about resale stores. The bargains on quality, barely used clothes are amazing.

•

276. They should know to not jump into the real estate market with an adjustable rate mortgage. A $900-a-month payment can balloon to an $1800-a-month payment and foreclosure in the blink of an eye.

277. They should know they won't
start out on their own living at
the standard their parents provided.
For many, this is a news flash.

•

278. They should know that if
they are afraid to open the bills,
it's time to stop spending.

•

279. They should know paying $200
for a pair of sneakers is something only
the dumb and uneducated do. Or adult
kids whose parents pay their bills.

280. They should know to never take an instant tax refund from anybody. The fee is a whopping 20 percent. And the government isn't *that* slow.

•

281. They should know a cell phone is cheaper than a landline, offers free long distance and free voice mail, and will always go wherever they do.

•

282. They should know that cool restaurants all over the city offer special dining deals. Just have to find them.

283. They should know to never, ever take a cash advance from one credit card to make a payment on another. This is the way losers live.

•

284. They should know used CDs are a much better deal than iTunes. And, hey, the truly industrious can resell them.

•

285. They should know having roommates saves big money. Just about everyone can learn to be agreeable.

•

286. They should know that basing their happiness on how they compare financially to their friends is a sure ticket to misery.

287. They should know people lived for thousands of years without a plasma TV. They can make it a couple of years.

•

288. They should know that making a budget won't only help them live within their means now, but give them a road map for wealth down the road.

•

289. They should know there are people making $250,000 a year who can't live within their means.

•

290. They should know to call a credit counseling service if their bills are out of hand.

291. They should know that many kids who move home don't save a dime. They just spend everything on cars, clothes, and partying. Kind of like high school.

•

292. They should know that one big secret to stretching money is living near one's work.

•

293. They should know the difference between a want and a need before they spend their money. For instance, they need a car that runs, not a new Beamer.

•

294. They should know to save something every month. Call it an emergency fund so they don't have to move home.

295. They should know to always deposit their paycheck in a bank and to never cash it at a check-cashing store. They may as well be dealing with the mob since they'll be paying mob rates.

•

296. They should know to not waste their money in a time-share condo. Just go on a vacation instead.

•

297. They should know customers of "payday" loan companies often pay up to 1000 percent of their loan value. This ensures the poor will remain poor.

•

298. They should know sometimes life takes working two jobs.

299. They should know low automobile insurance rates depend as much on their credit as their driving record.

•

300. They should know that delayed gratification will help them avoid a majority of financial issues.

•

301. They should know that if they spend all their money on nightclubs and impressing people, they'll quickly have an impressive amount of debt.

•

302. They should know that if they can't afford to pay cash, they can't afford it.

303. They should know using a credit card is, in reality, taking out a short-term, very high interest loan.

•

304. They should know credit cards cause them to spend future income on present-day wants. The solution is to want less.

•

305. They should know that even low-interest credit cards come with enrollment fees, inactivity fees, over-limit fees, balance-transfer fees as well as transaction fees. Outside of that, they're pretty much free.

306. They should know if they're one day late paying on a 0-percent-interest credit card, the interest could zoom to a breathtaking 18 percent. That doesn't just bite. It bites and sucks and is impossible to pay off with minimum monthly payments.

•

307. They should know that unless they pay twice the minimum monthly payment, credit card balances never really go away.

•

308. They should know the easiest way to gain control of their finances is to track their spending. Then they can make decisions on what to live without: imported beer? tanning salon? designer shoes?

309. They should know declaring bankruptcy after a MasterCard spending spree is not a spiritual option. They must pay their debts.

•

310. They should know credit union rates are usually better than the bank for borrowing and saving. Banks would prefer they not know this.

•

311. They should know to get a checking account with overdraft protection. No one's records are always perfect.

312. They should know balancing their account every month saves nasty surprises and overdraft charges—and involves sixth-grade math skills.

•

313. They should know to think of their bank statements as homework. There'll be long, confusing sentences. Addition and subtraction. And not doing it has consequences.

•

314. They should know debt collectors are just like them only with a worse job. And they'll deal.

315. They should know a debt collector can't say, "We'll take your house," or "We'll tell your boss," or "We'll tell your parents." And they can't demand payment that day.

•

316. They should know that every debt collector has to provide a copy of the loan, documentation proving who owns the loan, and a payment history. If the collector doesn't have that, treat it like a prank call.

•

317. They should know that one of the keys to good credit is continually monitoring their credit report. And raising heck when it's wrong.

318. They should know bankers want to get to know them even if their account is small. It's how bankers make money.

•

319. They should know banks aren't doing anybody any favors by making loans. So comparison shop even the good offers.

•

320. They should know to renew their warranties. Cars, computers, music players, and DVDs all break.

•

321. They should know ignoring their student loans will ruin their credit.

322. They should know they can build a good credit history without MasterCarding a dime. Get a small bank loan and put the proceeds into an interest bearing account that automatically pays the loan off every month.

•

323. They should know to set up automatic online payments for their regular monthly bills. It's a great invention for people who can't remember where they put the mail.

•

324. They should know that using a credit card to pile up travel awards works only if the credit card is paid in full every month. Failure to do so means really expensive "free" airline tickets.

325. They should know the unexpected happens every month. Sewers back up. Friends walk through glass doors. The old lady next door doesn't put her cigarette out. They need to budget for the unexpected too.

•

326. They should know that college loans can be consolidated, payment plans can be changed, and sometimes loans can be deferred. Just don't let payments pile up.

•

327. They should know there are interest-rate calculators all over the Internet to help them calculate the true cost of MasterCarding a $1,000 TV. (In some cases it can be up to five figures).

328. They should know a credit card company will often lower the interest rate of any customer in good standing who demands it. Just ask for a supervisor.

•

329. They should know that an ATM is as heartless as it is convenient. Kicking it won't magically produce funds. Only another deposit will.

•

330. They should know if they forget to take their ATM receipt, they could likely find their banking information posted on the Internet.

331. They should know banks will often reverse bad check charges when customers complain. Just not every month.

•

332. They should know checking accounts aren't free. People charge you to use your money. It's weird.

•

333. They should know one of the proven keys to prosperity is giving back to God even when there's not a lot to start with.

They Should Know Where "The Money" Is So They Don't Get Stuck in a Loser Career and Have to Move Home

Racking up $50,000 in student loans just to major in music appreciation doesn't make sense. *Money Magazine* and Salary.com listed the top fifty career choices based on salary and industry growth. They all require at least a bachelor's degree, they all have an average annual pay of over $50,000, and their fields are exploding.

•

334. Software Engineer

•

335. College Professor

•

336. Financial Adviser

337. Human Resources Manager

•

338. Physician's Assistant

•

339. Market Research Analyst

•

340. Computer/IT Analyst

•

341. Real Estate Appraiser

•

342. Pharmacist

•

343. Psychologist

•

344. Advertising Manager

345. Physical Therapist

•

346. Technical Writer

•

347. Chiropractor

•

348. Medical Scientist

•

349. Physical Scientist

•

350. Engineer

•

351. Curriculum Developer

•

352. Editor

353. Public Relations Specialist

•

354. Sales Manager

•

355. Optometrist

•

356. Property Manager

•

357. Actuary

•

358. Writer

•

359. Social Service Manager

•

360. Paralegal

361. Health Services Manager

•

362. Advertising Sales Agent

•

363. Physician/Surgeon

•

364. Management Analyst

•

365. Occupational Therapist

•

366. Mental Health Counselor

•

367. Landscape Architect

•

368. Biotechnology Research Scientist

369. Urban Planner

•

370. Lawyer

•

371. Speech-Language Pathologist

•

372. Meeting and Convention Planner

•

373. Dietitian/Nutritionist

•

374. Biological Scientist

•

375. Financial Analyst

•

376. Dentist

377. Accountant

•

378. Environmental Scientist

•

379. Lab Technologist

•

380. Registered Nurse

•

381. Sales Engineer

•

382. Veterinarian

•

383. School Administrator

They Should Know How to Locate and Conduct Themselves in Their First Apartment So They're Not Thrown Out and Have to Move Home

384. They should know that, in many cities, finding their first apartment can be as hard as finding their first job. Again, getting up off the couch is the key.

•

385. They should know to tell even the mail carrier they're looking for a apartment. You never know whose cousin's brother's aunt has a place.

•

386. They should know to not leave home without renters insurance. They're betting against the house without it. Literally.

387. They should know where
apartment deposits come from.
By working summer jobs.
A fact of life they may have missed.

•

388. They should know it's not
their parent's name going on the
lease contract. And they can't just
decide they don't like the small
closets after three months and split.

•

389. They should know to never
sign a long-term lease on a place
under major renovation that can't
be occupied on a specified date.

390. They should know to
never pay broker fees.

•

391. They should know to read
and understand their lease.
Don't sign and wonder.

•

392. They should know the date when
the lease officially starts. It could be on
the day of signing; it could be the day
they move in. Just get it in writing.

•

393. They should know their heating
rights. They have a right to be so warm
they can walk around in their underwear,
or the manager has to make concessions.

394. They should know that if more than a third of their salary goes to rent, they will miss out on a lot of a life.

•

395. They should know "No Pets Allowed" includes the puppy they just fell in love with. Fines are steep.

•

396. They should know that if they live in an apartment and work all day, they really don't even need to be buying a parakeet.

•

397. They should know to budget no more than one-fortieth of their annual income on monthly rent. That means if they're making $35,000 a year, they can afford $875 a month. Tops.

398. They should know many
apartments in the "coolest" parts
of town all but necessitate a
license to carry a gun after dark.

•

399. They should know their
apartment should be close to work,
or they'll get so sick of rush-hour
traffic they'll want to break the lease.

•

400. They should know to Google the
address of any place they're thinking about
renting. See what headlines come up.

•

401. They should know that unless
they find an apartment with utilities
included, they'll have to learn to turn off
the lights and turn down thermostats.

402. They should know to put off that plasma TV purchase until after they move in. Some leases require the renter to have a healthy savings account.

•

403. They should know apartment managers pull credit ratings. Anything under 620 essentially tells the management they're staring at a deadbeat.

•

404. They should know to visit with a couple of tenants to see how they like the place, if the management is responsive, and if the dudes upstairs dance all night.

405. They should know to not be so in love with the look of a place, they fail to ask about parking, pets, on-site management, maintenance, and laundry rooms. These are the things that will drive them nuts.

•

406. They should know to check out if the guy next door just looks creepy or actually *is* creepy. The site www.familywatchdog.us gives addresses of sex offenders.

407. They should know to make sure everything works before they sign: lights, toilet, oven, air conditioner, heater, stove, and showers. After they sign, management may not be responsible for repairs.

•

408. They should know to send change of address information to everybody they owe money to or who might send them money.

•

409. They should know to take pictures of anything broken or torn or scraped the day they move in. Doing it six months later will be unconvincing proof and may lead to loss of deposit.

410. They should know whether they
can sublet the apartment or not
and what the rules are for doing so.
It may be a way to leave the place
before the lease expires.

•

411. They should know to not make
a final decision on any apartment
until they plug in and turn on their hair
dryer along with all of the kitchen appliances and apartment lights. See how
long it takes to blow out the circuits.

•

412. They should know what happens
if they break the lease. It usually goes
under the title "Not Advisable."

413. They should know to not pay a dime to anyone until the lease is signed. They have the power of the pen.

•

414. They should know to get in writing who's responsible for repairing what. And if tenants are responsible for fighting off the roaches, repairing roof leaks, and fixing the electricity. They may want to reconsider.

•

415. They should know stupid roommates are expensive. There's property damage, unpaid rent, and accumulated fines they could find themselves responsible for.

416. They should know to disinfect every surface of the entire apartment the day they move in. And to not stop until their mother will touch things without rubber gloves.

•

417. They should know that the big, dark, ugly thing running around the silverware drawer is a roach, and he has thousands of drinking buddies. The National Guard would be of no help now.

•

418. They should know that living with a friend or a lover just might kill the whole relationship.

419. They should know that all apartments and condos have rules. And failure to follow those rules could mean getting tossed out on the street without a deposit refund.

•

420. They should know that in any apartment, water can be cut off, the power can go out, and sewers can back up. Stock up on candles, bottled water, and patience.

•

421. They should know that neighbors who aren't invited to their parties are often neighbors who will call the police.

422. They should know to give their elderly neighbors fair warning they are having people over who could be dancing and screaming at the top of their lungs. Ask them to call before they call the law.

•

423. They should know to not keep any bicycle they want to see again chained to a bike rack outside. Its days are numbered.

•

424. They should know neighbors can steal the signals off their high-speed wireless Internet. Pass-code everything. Or make a deal with the neighbors.

425. They should know they can furnish their apartment for a song at www.craigslist.com.

•

426. They should know somebody with a pickup truck. That way they can furnish their place by telling friends and family they'll pick up unwanted TVs, couches, and tables.

•

427. They should know to keep their lease accessible at all times. To see if the landlord is right, to see if the angry neighbors know what they're talking about, or to compare it to next year's lease.

428. They should know to shop IKEA for new furniture. Thirteen-year-olds can put this stuff together. College grads should be able to.

•

429. They should insist their friends not leave beer cans and cigarettes on neighbors' porches. And realize elderly neighbors have nothing to do except sit around and stew about how mad they are.

•

430. They should know to enforce a rule among their friends: nobody barfs in the common entryway.

•

431. They should know to be proud of their place. They're now home.

They Should Know How to Move Their Stuff So It Doesn't Get Broken or Lost and They Have to Move Home

432. They should know moving
causes about as much stress as a
job change, so don't freak out.
At least not more than three times.

•

433. They should know they need
boxes. Shoe boxes. Big boxes.
File boxes. Stuff has to go somewhere.

•

434. They should know to stock up on
fclt-tipped markers, packing paper, large
self-stick labels, box cutters, scissors,
packing peanuts, and packing tape.

•

435. They should know to start packing
early. Not the day of the move.

436. They should know to pack stuff like clothes, sheets, and towels in their suitcases. Easier to carry.

•

437. They should know to not pack stuff in the drawers of desks and bedside tables and dressers. Moving buddies will not be happy.

•

438. They should know to pack room by room. Toothbrushes and toothpaste thrown in with the stereo speakers can make every album sound like Michael Jackson.

439. They should know to label each box with the room where it needs to go. Or a box of kitchen utensils could wind up in the back of the coat closet.

•

440. They should know if they pack a box too full, the bottom will fall out. And it could be the box with the computer.

•

441. They should know to not cram so much stuff in the boxes, they can't lift them without popping an artery.

•

442. They should know books and magazines packed all together weigh a ton Enough to think twice about moving them.

443. They should know to move the stuff in the kitchen and fridge early. It saves a lot of time (and comes in handy when hunger strikes and thirst rules) on moving day.

•

444. They should know how to pack a truck if they're moving themselves. Basically, the heaviest stuff goes in first, right behind the driver.

•

445. They should know driving a truck is not the same as driving a car. One screwup will make movers look like a bargain.

446. They should know to have the utilities turned on the day before they move, or key things won't work: lights, air conditioning, appliances, water heater.

•

447. They should know one of the great things about a house-warming party is that friends will help unpack boxes as long as they can drink and eat.

They Should Know to Avoid Declaring Bankruptcy So They Don't Have to Move Home

448. They should know that most people facing bankruptcy are people who failed to live within their means.

•

449. They should know bankruptcy underscores a spiritual failure as much as it does a financial failure. Some amends will have to be made to those left holding the bag.

•

450. They should know that bankruptcy produces an extraordinary amount of stress, tension, headaches, digestive issues, sleep deprivation, and misery. And alcohol and drugs won't help.

451. They should know bankruptcy could impact their ability to rent an apartment.

•

452. They should know people who have declared bankruptcy pay the highest interest rates and fees out there because they are now high-risk borrowers.

•

453. They should know that bankruptcy will follow them around for seven to ten years and cost them thousands and thousands of dollars in higher interest payments.

•

454. They should know future car and home purchases will be almost impossible to finance.

455. They should know the necessities of life—cable TV, satellite radio, a new cell phone—won't be acquired without an enormous amount of hassle.

•

456. They should know that if they file Chapter 7, they will most probably be tossed out of their house or condo if they fall behind on payments.

•

457. They should know that once they file bankruptcy, they will spend the next decade rebuilding their credit score.

•

458. They should know prospective employers now pull credit reports. And regard a low credit score as the mark of a loon.

459. They should know bankruptcy doesn't mean they've beaten the system. They may still have to sell everything to pay off student loans, child support, and alimony.

•

460. They should know insurers would rather insure a prune than someone who has declared bankruptcy.

•

461. They should know there is no guarantee bankruptcy records can't be uncovered fifteen years later.

•

462. They should know they can often avoid bankruptcy by working out payment plans with the lender.

463. They should know to take every possible step to avoid bankruptcy: selling the new boat, the gold Rolex, the motor-cycle—and taking a second job. This kind of dire situation requires adult thinking.

•

464. They should know if they lie about their bankruptcy to get a loan, they've technically committed fraud.

•

465. They should know that if faced with a mountain of debts, pay off the smallest ones first. It builds momentum.

•

466. They should know to bring God into this situation. It's obviously time for Him to start directing their spending and saving.

They Should Know About Relationships So a Bad One Won't Force Them to Move Home

467. They should know failed relationships are one of the main reasons adult kids move home.

•

468. They should know to marry character.

•

469. They should know to not worry about being alone. God has plans.

•

470. They should know being alone is a good way to get to know oneself. (And if they don't like who they are, a relationship is doomed.)

471. They should know relationships are like anything else: they'll grow with a little love, a little watering, and not too much heat.

•

472. They should know that a person who smiles back at them isn't proposing marriage.

•

473. They should know to stay away from emotionally unavailable people who are afraid of commitment. Marriage won't make them any more available.

474. They should know that following someone, driving past their house, and posting things about them on the Internet indicates a need for therapy.

•

475. They should know when looking up prospects on the Internet, that just because someone says they're a single doctor doesn't mean they're not really a married chicken separator with eight kids.

•

476. They should know that if they can't invite God into the bedroom, then it's no place for them either.

477. They should know some people would rather work fifteen hours a day than go home to a person who loves them. And marrying them doesn't change them.

•

478. They should know that when they break up with somebody, not to continue to hang out with that person. Find new friends.

•

479. They should know to look up any prospective partner on MySpace or Facebook. If it looks like they're having sex with the Western world, keep looking.

480. They should know that seeking perfection in a mate will assure them of a lifetime of loneliness and disappointment.

•

481. They should know to never miss an opportunity to tell someone how important they are to them.

•

482. They should know they're no picnic to live with either.

•

483. They should know words can tear at a relationship as fast as actions.

•

484. They should know there's no biblical reason to wait for the other person to apologize first.

485. They should know to not spend more time on their wedding than on strengthening their relationship.
A lot of couples get it wrong here.

•

486. They should know if they are constantly walking on eggshells around another person, it's time to put on a new pair of running shoes. And flee.

•

487. They should know to not play house. Relationships should be kept sacred.

•

488. They should know sex produces babies. A lot of people forget this in the heat of the moment.

489. They should know there's an 85 percent chance of pregnancy if a sexually active couple doesn't use birth control, but only an 8 percent chance if a birth control pill is used properly.

•

490. They should know birth control devices aren't as easy to use as they think. Some even require practice.

•

491. They should know the pill can add to the risk of heart disease, high blood pressure, and blood clots. It can also cause nausea and increased appetite.

492. They should know most men have never had anyone show them how to use a condom correctly. Guess what that means.

•

493. They should know that over half of the women in their early twenties who have babies are unwed (LifeSiteNews.com).

•

494. They should know most single parents are mothers.

•

495. They should know that half of the unmarried women who give birth live below the poverty line.

496. They should know an
abortion will haunt both parents
for the rest of their lives.

•

497. They should know that if the
credit history of the person they're
engaged to is shaky, marriage won't
make them any more responsible.

•

498. They should know that many of
the longest lasting marriages have
started with the smallest of weddings.

•

499. They should know that when
compassion, forgiveness, kindness,
and gentleness leave a relationship,
love is not too far behind.

500. They should know that if a person breaks their heart time and again, it will happen again.

•

501. They should know to graduate from college before they get married.

•

502. They should know counseling for couples is a way to make sure everyone is grown-up enough to get married. A lot of churches offer this.

•

503. They should know the number one cause of divorce is finances.

•

504. They should know having kids does nothing to make a couple's finances better.

505. They should know a couple needs to get their expectations and realities on the same page before the marriage. Like, do they expect to live in a mansion on a teacher's salary?

•

506. They should know they can't change somebody by marrying them. Once screwy, always screwy.

•

507. They should learn the art of seeing the other point of view.

•

508. They should know old high-school friends are rarely welcome in an adult relationship.

509. They should know that women, by nature, deal with financial problems by reacting as if there were a nuclear attack. Men, by nature, react by watching football.

•

510. They should know to start saving for retirement the day after their honeymoon.

•

511. They should know the little everyday criticisms, bullying, and broken promises are what put a marriage on the road to Antarctica.

•

512. They should know that if they're in a failing relationship, they're not the victim. They're half the problem.

513. They should know that a strong marriage requires two strong people.

•

514. They should know to make the other feel appreciated and respected.

•

515. They should know that, curiously, people need to hear the words, "I love you" a lot. Even after the wedding.

•

516. They should know that fear poisons a marriage. And people get afraid when they feel powerless.

•

517. They should know to discuss the remote control. Men generally feel like they're giving up a body part when not holding it.

518. They should know they can either be happy or they can be right. People who are right all the time are single.

•

519. They should know marriage is like flying. Long stretches of soaring through the clouds...interrupted by moments of holding on to your stomach.

•

520. They should know the most intimate act a couple can do together is pray together.

•

521. They should know that once they get married, God has an interest in seeing them stay married.

522. They should know that trust is one of those curious things that, when lost, is hard to find again.

•

523. They should know to not focus on the other person's faults. Or the list of faults will keep getting longer.

•

524. They should know if they feel a need to control someone else's mood, degree of happiness, amount of drinking, or level of fear, what they really need is a good 12-step program.

•

525. They should know we all need someone to miss us.

526. They should know that there is no excuse for abuse in a relationship.

•

527. They should know that if someone says, "I have an emotional wall I put up to keep from getting hurt," they're dealing with a loon. Move on.

•

528. They should know successful relationships are based on common values, shared morals, and good old-fashioned commitment.

•

529. They should know that no relationship should force them to compromise their principles or self-respect.

530. They should know most couples would rather stick needles in their eyes than talk about finances and sex. And both need to be talked about.

•

531. They should know making a budget is one of the most important things a couple can do. Before marriage.

•

532. They should know to not let a wedding put them in debt. One night of memories for five years of payments doesn't make sense.

533. They should know that by registering with World Vision's Alternative Wedding Gift List, they'd lose the matching silverware, but enable their friends to restore a person's sight or bring water to a village in Uganda.

•

534. They should know if they're fighting about money, they need to start talking about it.

•

535. They should know to pay bills together. It holds the fear down.

536. They should know to pay themselves every month. It's how couples retire in their fifties.

•

537. They should know to set financial goals: pay off the credit cards, save for a down payment on a home, put money aside for a vacation to Europe.

•

538. They should know to not confuse emotional intimacy with sexual intimacy. Sex has nothing to do with feeling respected, admired, worthy, and loved.

539. They should know the hardest part about saving a troubled marriage is recognizing and acknowledging it's in trouble in the first place.

•

540. They should know if people don't find emotional intimacy in a relationship, they might look for it someplace else.

•

541. They should know prayer strengthens a relationship. But prayer without action is nothing.

542. They should know that one key to wealth is a long-lasting marriage.

·

543. They should know a marriage is like a bank account: you're either making deposits or taking withdrawals.

·

544. They should know that after the "bloom" wears off, love is a decision.

·

545. They should know to be faithful.

·

546. They should know to stay and work it out.

They Should Know How to Live Without Mom Waking Them Up, Doing Their Laundry, and Taking Care Of Them or Else They'll Move Home.

547. They should know that the inability to keep a home orderly and clean is a clear sign of someone who still needs mothering.

•

548. They should know how to separate and wash their clothes so they don't have to take them home.

•

549. They should know to invest in an ironing board. It will keep them from starting a fire on the breakfast table and moving home.

550. They should know bleach is really good at making things white. Even things that aren't white.

•

551. They should know that dirty dishes that sit around for days are havens for bacteria.

•

552. They should know to smell their refrigerator once a week and throw out the five-day-old Chinese leftovers.

•

553. They should know vacuuming doesn't wear out a carpet. Dirt and grime wear out a carpet. Vacuuming actually makes it last longer.

554. They should know that mold and mildew are evidence their place is becoming a toxic dump.

•

555. They should know that roaches and ants are usually invited in by food lying around on the floor and counters.

•

556. They should know the great thing about the dishwasher is that it can be used to clean toothbrushes, oven vents, knobs, hairbrushes, trays—anything that's bacteria laden, gross, and fits inside.

557. They should know 95 percent
of the indoor dirt comes from
porches, sidewalks, and entryways.
They start sneezing, they think
they have the flu, and they come home.

•

558. They should know to use doormats.
A pound of dirt is often found there.

•

559. They should know that
when their apartment starts
smelling, it's time to disinfect.

•

560. They should know human
hair wreaks havoc on drains.

561. They should know to put everything back in the refrigerator. And not eat anything that's been lying out for three days.

•

562. They should know that, if left undisturbed, dust will only grow.

•

563. They should know a dirty apartment can make them sick.

•

564. They should know to buy a loud, obnoxious alarm clock with a snooze button. They have to get up a 6 a.m now.

•

565. They should know who to call in case of an emergency. Besides Mom.

566. They should know washing hands with soap and hot water has stopped plagues. It can stop anything lurking in their apartment.

•

567. They should know those little red bumps spreading across their skin aren't the result of too much chocolate.

•

568. They should know when they're blowing snot, coughing, feeling feverish, and having trouble breathing, partying all night is rarely the recommended course of treatment.

•

569. They should know the word *generic* can save them a fortune.

570. They should know calling Mom when they're sick will only get them sympathy. Calling a doctor will get them a prescription.

•

571. They should know that when they run at sunrise or sunset, they're running with mosquitoes carrying diseases. Spray with OFF! first.

•

572. They should know to sit across the room from people who are coughing. Even their friends.

•

573. They should know the people with the best tans usually have skin cancer surgery first.

574. They should know surgical scars really ruin a tan line, and more young people are getting skin cancer than ever before.

•

575. They should know tanning beds—surprise!!!—cause skin cancer.

•

576. They should know those chewable multivitamins they took when they were six years old are still good for them.

•

577. They should know if they have to suck in their stomach to button their buttons, they just might need to start exercising.

578. They should know if they stop drinking, they will instantly feel better.

•

579. They should know having something for breakfast besides a doughnut and a Coke will make them smarter.

•

580. They should know an apple in the morning is a more effective wakeup than caffeine. Unless, of course, they're addicted to caffeine.

•

581. They should know that if they make a habit of eating when they're really happy or really sad, they're really in trouble.

582. They should know it's more
likely for an overweight person to
gain even more weight than to lose any.

•

583. They should know that anything
"supersized" is too much food.

•

584. They should know sharing
meals is one way thin people stay thin.

•

585. They should know secondhand
mattresses come with a bonus. Bedbugs.

•

586. They should know that
volunteering cures loneliness.

587. They should know too much partying can lead to exhaustion, depression,
miserable job or school performance,
and strange sores all over their body.

•

588. They should know that keeping
things like Band-Aids around will
save their clothes and furniture.

•

589. They should know that if
they needed ADD medicine in high
school, their employer, fellow
employees, and friends would be
grateful if they kept taking it.

590. They should know a marathoner doesn't need any more protein than a couch potato. (It's wild how protein-consuming changing channels is.)

•

591. They should know missing meals is not a good way to lose weight. It's a good way to get so ravenous, chocolate is consumed all night.

•

592. They should know that using someone else's razor means taking something sharp with staph on it and scraping it against their skin. Good luck with that.

593. They should know to get their teeth examined regularly. All kinds of activities are going on in their mouth.

•

594. They should know there's no real reason for anyone under forty years old to have anything to do with a plastic surgeon.

•

595. They should know to not go around blowing their nose on napkins or sleeves. Carry tissues or handkerchiefs.

•

596. They should know used, snotty tissue piled up on the floor or bed is essentially a toxic waste dump.

597. They should know that if they don't eat their fiber now, they'll be drinking Metamucil very soon.

•

598. They should know that bad hygiene frequently results in body odor, antibiotics, and people not wanting to approach them.

•

599. They should know most of the world's truly successful people wake up before everyone else.

•

600. They should know it's more important to wake up at the same time every morning than go to bed at the same time every night.

601. They need to know their body will
pay them back for ingesting drinks like
Red Bull to keep the late-night party going.

•

602. They should know their ability
to eat sixteen times a day and nap all
afternoon without gaining an ounce
will disappear soon. (This is
what happened to their parents.)

•

603. They should know what pills
to take for what. Antibiotics don't
work for relieving a headache.

•

604. They should know it's easier
to keep nausea and first-aid medicine
around before it's needed rather
than drive to the drug store or their
parents' while barfing out the window.

605. They should know high-fiber food like fruits and veggies and whole grains will keep them out of the doctor's office.

•

606. They should know pizza— while it does contain protein, dairy, bread, and sometimes vegetables— isn't a perfect food to be eaten every day.

•

607. They should know they won't lose a pound running three miles a day unless they give up the ice cream, beer, chips, Coke, and doughnuts.

•

608. They should know the addition of fluoride in water reduces cavities. And fluoride on a toothbrush produces the same miracle.

609. They should know soap can actually make a bathroom dirty and unhealthy and in dire need of disinfecting.

•

610. They should know to examine what new things are growing on their toothbrush before they stick it in their mouth.

•

611. They should know a thermometer isn't a swizzle stick.

•

612. They should know how to take their temperature. Because that's the first question their doctor and mother will ask them.

613. They should know to go to a doctor the moment their eyes are leaking weird things or their vision is turning blurry.

•

614. They should know one of the upsides to eating healthy is that it's cheaper than fast food.

•

615. They should know smoking, alcohol, fatty foods, and not moving off the couch all seem like a fun lifestyle . . . until one is forty and can't get off the couch.

•

616. They should know constant worrying can lead young people to develop shingles, a nasty condition that causes sores inside as well as outside the body.

617. They should know they'll
need to deal with stressful issues.
Not just hope they'll go away.

•

618. They should know they're
getting older. Health screenings,
checkups, and good hygiene can
keep things from going south.

•

619. They should know that no matter
how good looking the other person is,
if they're sneezing, wiping their nose,
and coughing up phlegm, they're toxic.

620. They should know that although throwing up, starving oneself, smoking and taking speed all help lose weight, nobody wants to hang out with a jumpy, smelly, skittish half dead person.

•

621. They should know a nice smile will take them farther in life than new clothes. Pick a dentist over a new wardrobe.

•

622. They should know flossing helps gums, teeth, heart, and breath.

•

623. They should know allergies won't kill them. They'll just make them feel like they're dying.

624. They should know if they can't read a street sign, it's time for an eye exam.

•

625. They should know disinfecting bathrooms, bathtubs, showers, kitchens, handles, and doorknobs every week isn't paranoia. It's why the human race continues to exist.

•

626. They should know to not use the hospital emergency room for minor stuff. It takes hours to be seen, costs a small fortune, and is filled with really sick, toxic people.

627. They should know how to clean
and dress a wound. Boy Scouts
and Camp Fire Girls know this.

•

628. They should know to not put
anything between their lips that is on fire.

•

629. They should know that things like
stress, hormones, and vitamin deficien-
cies increase the outbreak of zits.
Antibiotics can clear them.

•

630. They should know green tea is hip.
And comes both caffeinated and
decaffeinated. And reportedly reduces
the risk of cancer, heart disease,
cholesterol, and infection. And it's cheaper
than espresso drinks. And at Starbucks.

631. They should know to not believe anyone who says, "It's just a cold sore."

•

632. They should know to close the lid before flushing. Especially if toothbrushes and washrags are sitting nearby.

•

633. They should know to treat any hot tub as a toxic germ factory. Unless they've personally cleaned and disinfected it.

•

634. They should know to not exercise in any air they can see. Smog, smoke, and dust will kill you as fast as inactivity.

They Should Know the Secrets of Home Repair and Home Depot So When Something Breaks, They Won't Move Home

635. They should know to get a home warranty when buying a home or condo. Everything breaks.

•

636. They should know that what their parents didn't teach them about home repair, a book can.

•

637. They should know a leaky roof, an overflowing toilet, and a clogged sink are part of life. God doesn't have it out for them.

•

638. They should know that home repair is all about being brave enough to make mistakes. And knowing when to call a professional.

639. They should know they won't look like a fool by walking into a Home Depot and announcing they don't know what they need, how to install it, or where it goes. They'll look like a customer.

•

640. They should know it's easy to lose focus in a Home Depot. Don't go in looking for a socket wrench and leave with a riding lawn mower.

•

641. They should know that before they buy a new fridge, first pull the cover plate off their old one and vacuum the coils.

642. They should know dryer vents holding three pounds or more of lent are a fire hazard. And gross.

•

643. They should know to regularly examine the shower floor and see if anything on it is mating. Clorox helps here. A year's worth is dirt cheap.

•

644. They should know home repair requires the right tools. A drill is of no value when installing a garbage disposal.

645. They should know how to turn the
water off from behind the toilet.
They'll want to know this before
the toilet begins to back up.

•

646. They should know to make sure their
chimney vents are open before lighting a
fire. Smoke needs somewhere to go
besides the living room.

•

647. They should know it's cheaper to get
things inspected than to buy new. Plus,
Home Depot doesn't sell furnaces or
central air conditioning systems.

648. They should know taking home repair classes at Lowe's or Home Depot is like taking shop in high school. Only without the hoods.

THEY TEACH MILLIONS OF THINGS LIKE:

•

649. How to get organized

•

650. How to use power tools

•

651. How to install track lighting

•

652. How to install a ceiling fan without doing bodily damage

•

653. How to install a new toilet without damaging the house

654. How to prep and paint interior walls and trim

•

655. How to use a pressure washer (What man or woman doesn't want to know this?)

•

656. How to update kitchen cabinets and fixtures

•

657. They should know air conditioning filters are really cheap at Home Depot. Around $5.

•

658. They should know that when the wind is blowing through the windows, it's time to invest in eight-dollar-a-tube silicone caulk.

659. They should know the best way
to avoid home-repair scams is to never
hire anybody who calls them, e-mails
them, or shows up at their doorstep.
Legitimate companies are too busy
working to do these things.

•

660. They should know a crack in
the wall less than two inches wide
is the easiest thing to repair.
And a new water hose from the
hardware store can help prevent it.

•

661. They should know that if
they don't get approval for planned
improvements with their condo
association or apartment managers,
they can be tossed out on their tush.

662. They should know putting off small repairs can have big consequences. Like a hole in the roof that's a fifteen-minute job versus dealing with a flood in the attic that ruins everything and isn't covered by insurance.

•

663. They should know there are certain things you never put in the garbage disposal: cantaloupe rinds, eggshells, raw meat, tamale husks. Bird seed isn't recommended either.

664. They should know how that
if they do insist on testing the
limits of the garbage disposal, they'll
need to learn how to use a plumber's
snake. Found in the plumbing
department near the plungers.

•

665. They should know to never mix
ammonia with bleach. Wars have been
fought with less lethal gases.

•

666. They should know that before
they do anything to a clogged drain, try
a liquid drain opener. It's simple, easy
to use, and doesn't involve tools.

667. They should know to remember this rule of home repair: good materials are never cheap, and cheap materials are never good. Refusal to admit this is why smart people buy stock in home repair stores.

•

668. They should know all good repairs start with a budget and planning. Or a $50 home repair job can balloon to $500 before the paint dries.

•

669. They should know a basic truth to home repair is that it's always twice as expensive as planned and takes twice as long.

670. They should know to have all their tools and materials together before starting a job. The alternative is to create a mess, not have the stuff to fix it, run out of time, live in a pigpen, call Mom for help, and then move home.

•

671. They should know that, before investing a fortune in routers, saws, and electric nail guns, get lessons first.

•

672. They should know that while some hardware salespeople might know the nuances of the National Electric Code, others might not recognize a Phillips head screwdriver when they see one.

673. They should know that if they can't find lessons for doing a specific repair, the Internet is free and has unlimited information. And there are pictures.

•

674. They should know there are times to call an expert. Like when installing gas lines. The whole neighborhood will be grateful.

•

675. They should know failure to get the required permits from the local building department means the most expensive construction can be stopped.

676. They should know the best
way to never see their contractor
again is pay him in full before the
job is finished. Dole it out.

•

677. They should know the most
impact for their home repair dollar
is in the kitchen and bathroom.

•

678. They should know that, just
by itself, a paint job works
wonders for sprucing up a place.

•

679. They should know painting is a
bit more complicated than just buying a
can of paint and a brush. Ask for help.

680. They should know to not spend a fortune on tools. It's better to rent them— and spend a fortune on materials instead.

•

681. They should know safety goggles, hard hats, gloves, and nail pouches will help keep them out of the emergency room.

•

682. They should know the worst time to get a simple question answered in a hardware store is on the weekends. That's when millions of other do-it-yourselfers are wandering around with questions.

•

683. They should know to test their smoke alarm.

684. They should know a fire extinguisher can keep a small kitchen fire from forcing them to move home.

•

685. They should know the last thing to use on an electrical fire is water. That's when you run and call 911.

•

686. They should know that if their circuits are blowing out nightly, it's either the hair dryer or they're living in a firetrap.

•

687. They should know running water through all their drains once a month is a cheap, effective way to know if a hair ball is building up.

They Should Know How to Buy and Maintain a Car So They Don't Spend $50,000 on a Junker and Have to Move Home

688. They should know consumerreports.org rates every car manufactured since 1997. They can learn if a car's beauty is only skin deep.

•

689. They should know www.carbuyingtips.com can help them get their credit report, secure loan approval, get competing dealer quotes, find the best price on new car warranties, and even help them prepare offer sheets for dealers.

•

690. They should know to have financing and loan approvals ready before they walk into a dealership. It's called ammunition.

691. They should know that MSRP
is the base retail price of a car before
all the fees are rolled in. Dealer cost is
what the dealer actually paid for the car.
The difference is whether the dealer
vacations in Maui or Galveston.

•

692. They should know to make sure
to get an MSRP if they buy the car.
It's their guarantee that the features
they paid for are actually on the car.

•

693. They should know the sticker
price is fantasyland. Ignore it.

694. They should know buying
a good used car can save them
thousands of dollars over a new one.
Assuming they do their homework
and get background checks.

•

695. They should know to establish
their budget before going car shopping.
Some hot red sports car could make
them forget rent is due on the first.

•

696. They should know the goal of dealer
newspaper ads is to get people into the
dealer. Not sell the cars advertised.

697. They should know what they need a vehicle to do. Haul bricks? Commute to work in the next town? Drive two hundred highway miles daily? Impress the opposite sex?

•

698. They should know there are over two million car accidents a year, so there's a good chance the used car they're looking at has been in one of them.

•

699. They should know there's a difference between a fender bender in the parking lot and a car that has been hit by a semi. One might be a good buy; the other, years of headaches.

700. They should know there's
a price for being cool. When gas
prices rise, it can cost over $200
a month just to fuel certain cars.

•

701. They should know buying a
car is like dating: it's easy to be
fooled by looks alone. Get a vehicle
history report at CarFax.com
or ConsumerGuide.com
even on new-looking cars.

•

702. They should know what
the word *certified* means
before they buy a used car.

703. They should know to be
skeptical of odometer readings.
Someone could make the car appear
barely broken in when in reality
it was driven into the ground.
Another reason to pull a history report.

•

704. They should know a number of
used cars out there have been salvaged,
stolen, or recalled. Salespeople may
not tell them this. Car histories do.

•

705. They should know a car history
would tell them if the car has ever
failed inspection. In the car business,
once a failure, always a failure.

706. They should know where the car came from. If it came from the Louisiana or Mississippi coasts, there's a good chance it was flooded. And is worthless.

•

707. They should know even the worst air conditioner seems to work well in the winter. How well does it work in August?

•

708. They should know to not buy any used car before their mechanic puts it on a lift and gives it a full vehicle inspection.

•

709. They should know to not argue with the mechanic who finds something wrong with their beloved car. And not to be stupid and buy it anyway.

710. They should know to never, ever buy a car and sign an "AS IS" statement. That means the engine could fall out the moment they leave the lot, and, well, they're screwed.

•

711. They should know what experts think the car is worth before they buy it. Places to check are the NADA Official Used Car Guide, Kelly Blue Book, or Consumer Reports Used Car Buying Guide. Their friends' opinions are worthless.

•

712. They should know to demand a thirty-day money-back guarantee in writing. If the dealer says no, leave the car alone.

713. They should know their credit
score before they walk into a dealership.
It's free at Experian.com and will
keep a dealer from socking them
with a higher interest rate.

•

714. They should know that even
though they think of themselves
as convertible people, the best car
for them might be a minivan.

•

715. They should know *APR* means
"annual percentage rate," and
it's different for different people.

716. They should know that if their credit score is over 680, they'll qualify for the best loans. If their credit score is under 680, they'll be charged a higher APR.

•

717. They should know that if their credit score is under 550, they don't need a car. They need to repair their credit. This is when the sins of fast living on credit are paid for.

•

718. They should know that if their credit score is below six hundred, then any application they make will be rejected and will lower their score even further. It's not fair, but it's life.

719. They should know creditors
who have given them black marks
on their credit score can sometimes
be sweet-talked into removing
them. Worth a phone call.

•

720. They should know lenders don't like
people who move a lot. Stay in one place
at least six months before applying.

•

721. They should know that they
can pull their own credit report
without lowering their credit score.
Some car dealers will say otherwise.

722. They should know to keep their credit balances below 50 percent of their credit limit or their credit score will be lowered. Strange, but true.

•

723. They should know the absolutely lowest financing rates are found online, at sites like Capital One Auto Finance and E-LOAN. Takes ten minutes.

•

724. They should know a car dealer will often quote them a lower monthly payment than E-LOAN, but it's for seventy-two months, not thirty-six. Wear protective gear when handling dealers.

725. They should know that if the dealer has stuck them with a large APR because "they couldn't get into a car otherwise," they should refinance it. Go online to E-LOAN or Capital One Auto Finance and save big.

•

726. They should know that zero-percent financing doesn't apply to everybody. Only those with good credit scores.

•

727. They should know the difference between a three-year loan and six-year loan can be thousands of dollars in interest.

728. They should know that if they allow the bank to automatically debit their car loan every month, they'll get an even lower APR.

•

729. They should know how to compare the difference between low interest financing and a $3000 rebate. Higher level math.

•

730. They should know one way to avoid negotiation hassles is to get price quotes from Cars.com, CarsDirect, and InvoiceDealers and e-mail them to five dealers. See if anyone accepts.

731. They should know that, at the end of the month, dealers would sell their mother to sell a car. By the end of the year, they're eyeing their first born.

•

732. They should know the secret to buying a hot-selling new car is patience. Car dealers count on a buyer's impatience.

•

733. They should know to leave their checkbook and credit cards at home when shopping at a dealer the first time. The dealer's job is to not let them leave without a car.

734. They should know four words when dealing with automobile dealers: get it in writing. As far as the law is concerned, if it's not in writing, it was never said.

•

735. They should know to compare prices found on the Internet with local dealers. Dealers aren't fond of this idea, but they'll match lower prices.

•

736. They should know to not rave about a car while test-driving it with a salesperson. The price won't go up, but the pressure to close a deal that day will.

737. They should know there's
no such thing as a one time price
to buy a car. Dealers don't make
money turning down offers
they made two weeks earlier.

•

738. They should know to look
past the incentives to reliability
and fuel economy. That's
where the true price lies.

•

739. They should know experts recom-
mend building a notebook of facts for
quick reference when negotiating with
a dealer. It levels the playing field.

740. They should know what to include their notebook: car quotes from other dealers and the Internet; quotes on financing, options, and warranties; and their credit report, credit score, and approved credit limit. Pull these out slowly. Let the dealer wonder what else is in there.

•

741. They should know a fair price for any car is dealer's cost plus 5 percent. Dealers may say it's not fair. It's fair. Whip out the notebook.

•

742. They should know to not be afraid of negotiations. They have the power if they've done their homework.

743. They should know to never make their trade-in part of the car-buying deal. That's a separate deal. The reason is, dealers can hide hundreds of dollars in fees and markups when the two deals are combined into one.

•

744. They should know that if their old car is in demand, they can sell it themselves on CarsDirect.com or Cars.com for up to $5000 more than the dealer will pay.

•

745. They should know to never tell a dealer what they can pay per month. That gives a dealer license to add fees, markups, and profits.

746. They should know "upside-down on a loan" means more is owed on a car than it's worth, possibly thousands of dollars more. People who need to sell but can't afford to for three or four years move home.

•

747. They should know to never trade in a car that they are upside-down on. It just means they'll be even more upside-down on the next one.

•

748. They should know the coolest, newest, never-before-seen cars come with bugs. Wait till the second year to buy. After the bugs are worked out.

749. They should know to not test drive a car with dents and dings before filling out a form with the business manager listing the defects. Or they could be stuck paying for them.

•

750. They should know that when the salesperson is pounding the calculator, a lot of this is for show. Let him pound.

•

751. They should know that when one salesperson leaves and another one comes in, this is the time to go. They're about to be played.

752. They should know that if they don't like to negotiate, they can make an offer to the salesperson and then leave. Let the dealer stew.

•

753. They should know to make sure all the fees a dealer adds during closing line up with car pricing sites. If the fee looks out of line, cross it out.

•

754. They should know that if a salesperson says he doesn't know what a certain fee is for, get up and leave. They're dealing with either an idiot or a liar.

755. They should know a new
car plummets in value the moment
it's driven off the lot. This creates
that upside down feeling.

•

756. They should know long-term car
loans on expensive cars mean they'll be
upside-down for a long time. And
screwed if they need to get rid of it.

•

757. They should know one way
to avoid being upside-down is to
plunk 20 percent down at closing.
That way the loan value will always
stay pretty much near the car value.

758. They should know that if the car is wrecked or stolen, insurance companies don't pay what is owed on the car, but what it's worth. One may owe $18,000 on a car worth only $15,000. That's called "the gap."

•

759. They should know to purchase "gap" insurance if they put less than 20 percent down. Dealers sell gap insurance, but it's much, much cheaper at www.gapinsurancequotes.com.

760. They should know to Google "online auto insurance" and learn the cost of insuring their car before buying it. In many cases, the cost of insurance is the deal killer on that spiffy five-speed sports car.

•

761. They should know a twenty-four-year-old single male will pay significantly more to insure a Corvette than a forty-year-old married female English teacher will pay to insure a Toyota.

•

762. They should know to buy uninsured motorist coverage. Most of the goobers out there who hit people don't have liability insurance.

763. They should know a car lease is just like a car loan: they are obligated to pay it off. They can't just get out of it because their once too-cool-to-live-without convertible has a rattle.

•

764. They should know anything longer than a sixty-month car lease is for suckers. At four years things start to break down, warranties expire, car repair gets expensive, and they're still upside-down on the lease.

•

765. They should know the best sales-person in the dealership is the finance manager. Their job is to sell $3,500 worth of stuff that costs only $500.

766. They should know that their goal with the finance manager is to pay the negotiated price for the car. Nothing else.

•

767. They should know the dealer will make more profit on a car's options than on the car. And most every option can be bought on the aftermarket for a fraction of the price.

•

768. They should know the main reason to turn down dealer financing is dealers can jack up the financed price with hidden charges on fees, warranties, and window etching.

769. They should know that while dealers will charge up to $800 to etch an auto's VIN number on the car window (to save on insurance), owners can do it themselves for less than $25. Go to www.vinetcher.com.

•

770. They should know that when the finance dealer tries to sell them "rust proofing," turn it down.

•

771. They should know the $300 "fabric protection" can be duplicated by using two cans of ScotchGuard. Turn it down.

772. They should know any dealer-prep charges are pure, unearned profit. Turn them down too.

•

773. They should know some dealers have been known to miscalculate the sales tax and actually mark up state fees and taxes. If this happens, leave.

•

774. They should know if their car is stolen, life will take on a new misery. Police are swamped, insurance drags its feet, car payments still have to be made, and money gets tighter. Home beckons.

775. They should know the manufacturer's warranty is peace of mind for about fifty thousand miles. An extended warranty costs extra, but it's peace of mind for one hundred thousand miles.

•

776. They should know to follow the manufacturer's warranty maintenance schedule. It's a minor hassle, but a broken down car that doesn't qualify for warranty coverage is a huge hassle.

•

777. They should know cars seem to break down the week after the manufacturer's warranty ends. That's what makes extended warranties important.

778. They should know that no
matter what dealers say, dealers
don't sell the best extended warranties.
Actually, dealers don't sell the
best of anything. Except cars.

•

779. They should know there are two
kinds of extended warranties: wear and
tear, and breakdown. Dealers generally
offer an expensive breakdown policy while
most claims are actually wear and tear.

•

780. They should know to shop
www.Warrantydirect.com for
extended warranties that are a
whopping 60 percent cheaper than
a dealer may charge. And they would
cover wear and tear *and* breakdown.

781. They should know a zero-deductible warranty costs more, but it means a covered repair will never cost them a dime.

•

782. They should know that if they buy an extended warranty on a used car, not to claim anything for sixty days or their file will be red-flagged. Not fair, but life.

•

783. They should know they'll never understand the wording of the dealer's extended warranty. A lawyer might. Maybe.

784. They should know that getting the oil changed every four thousand miles is what responsible adults do to keep their cars running smoothly.

•

785. They should know that if they're in a wreck, they have the right to choose their repair shop, no matter what the insurance company says.

They Should Have an Adult's Vocabulary So They Don't Sound Like a Teenager and Have to Move Home

786. The American Heritage® Dictionary has compiled a list of one hundred words every high-school graduate should know. This kind of vocabulary beats "Hey you," "Whatever," and "Pimp my ride" every time. And gets one hired.

abjure • abrogate • abstemious acumen • antebellum • auspicious belie • bellicose • bowdlerize chicanery • chromosome • churlish circumlocution • circumnavigate deciduous • deleterious • diffident enervate • enfranchise • epiphany equinox • euro • evanescent • expurgate

239

facetious • fatuous • feckless • fiduciary
filibuster • gamete • gauche
gerrymander • hegemony • hemoglobin
homogeneous • hubris • hypotenuse
impeach • incognito • incontrovertible
inculcate • infrastructure • interpolate
irony • jejune • kinetic • kowtow
laissez faire • lexicon • loquacious
lugubrious • metamorphosis • mitosis
moiety • nanotechnology • nihilism
nomenclature • nonsectarian • notarize
obsequious • oligarchy • omnipotent
orthography • oxidize • parabola

paradigm • parameter • pecuniary
photosynthesis • plagiarize • plasma
polymer • precipitous • quasar
quotidian • recapitulate • reciprocal
reparation • respiration • sanguine
soliloquy • subjugate • suffragist
supercilious • tautology • taxonomy
tectonic • tempestuous
thermodynamics • totalitarian
unctuous • usurp • vacuous • vehement
vortex • winnow • wrought
xenophobe • yeoman • ziggurat

They Should Know How to Get So Rich, Their Parents Can Move In with Them

787. They should know the first thing they do with their paycheck isn't to go out and put a down payment on a BMW. Now, BMW stock is another matter.

•

788. They should know if they use their money to change the world, God will curiously make sure they will wind up with more than they need.

•

789. They should know to put their cash in a money market account, not a CD. The rates are similar, but a CD will charge a fee to take money out.

790. They should know to never fall so much in love with a home that they ignore an inspection's negative findings.

•

791. They should know where their money is, where it's going, and how to get it. Always.

•

792. They should know to balance their financial books. Even if, years later, an accountant does their books for them.

•

793. They should know one trick of the wealthy is to deposit something from every paycheck into a 401(k). Years later, they'll have a small fortune.

794. They should know that if an employer offers a matching 401(k) program, that's free money. Every dollar invested automatically doubles.

•

795. They should know these three words: *get rich slowly*. Works every time.

•

796. They should know to invest with their eyes wide open— markets crash, gold dives, real estate tumbles.... There's no sure thing.

797. They should know delayed gratification is how some school teachers retire with millions of dollars in savings. They're buying stocks and real estate while everyone else is buying Jags and big screen TVs.

•

798. They should know if they start saving in their twenties, they only have to regularly put aside 10 percent of their paycheck to accumulate all the money they'll need for retirement.

•

799. They should know people with savings goals reach them. People without goals yank out the credit cards.

800. They should know a fifteen-year mortgage will save them a fortune compared to a thirty-year mortgage.

•

801. They should know about savings bonds. They're liquid and guaranteed to appreciate. They pay better than a savings account, and—depending on the world's situation—can be a great investment.

•

802. They should know their first financial goal is to accumulate the down payment for a house. Their second goal is to pay off the house.

803. They should know accumulating property is a hassle. You have to deal with tenants and repairmen and sometimes lawyers, but you can retire early. Really, really early.

•

804. They should know investing one dollar a day for thirty years at a 10 percent interest rate nets $67,000 at the end of thirty years.

•

805. They should know to contribute as much as they are allowed into their 401(k) plan every year.

806. They should know that compound interest can help them accumulate a fortune. It's how credit card companies make so much money.

•

807. They should know that before buying any real estate, they should get their own broker. Don't use the seller's.

•

808. They should know financial experts can help. Even the ones on radio and TV.

•

809. They should know that if they're day-trading, they're playing against the experts.

810.   They should know that buying a home or condo takes delayed gratification, living below your means, and a determined wealth accumulation.

•

811. They should know that words like *certificate of deposit, interest-bearing accounts, savings bonds, Dow Jones,* and *tax shelters* are now considered very sexy to say.

•

812. They should know to never believe a stock tip that arrives in their e-mail.

•

813. They should know buying stocks of large companies and holding them for decades is a time-honored way to accumulate money.

814. They should know the proven keys to long-term prosperity are making a budget, learning to live without, and regularly giving back to God. Prosperity has nothing to do with a large salary.

•

815. They should know that lenders are not their friends. They are cold, hard businesspeople who want their money back. With interest.

•

816. They should know wealth is a tool to further God's plans.

They Should Know What Gets the FBI and IRS So Mad at Them, They Have to Hide Out and Move Home

817. They should know easy
money usually results in hard time.

•

818. They should know that while
they've worked hard for their money,
the IRS wants its share. Now.

•

819. They should know to claim their
winnings from their last trip to
Las Vegas. The IRS knows about them.
The IRS knows everything.

•

820. They should know filing too
many exemptions is just like
stamping their return with
a big red "AUDIT ME" stamp.

821. They should know if the
IRS doesn't like a certain deduction
they've taken, penalties follow.

•

822. They should know you can go
to jail for not declaring income.

•

823. They should know if they
withdraw money from a 401(k) plan,
they are subject to a 10 percent federal
penalty. Claim it. Don't try to hide it.

•

824. They should know the tax structure
for a self-employed person is too
complex to not use a CPA or tax adviser.

825. They should know the IRS garnishes wages to collect back taxes. Meaning their landlord will soon toss them. Meaning they'll be home.

•

826. They should know the IRS can levy bank and savings accounts at their choosing. This is called "being in hot water."

•

827. They should know that even if they file for an extension to send in their 1040, they have to actually pay their taxes by April 15.

828. They should know that it takes something like a stage-five hurricane to get a six-month extension on paying their taxes. And even then the IRS doesn't get too sentimental.

•

829. They should know that if they can't pay their taxes on time, they're toast. They need to work out an installment agreement with the IRS quickly or get a bank loan.

•

830. They should know the number one reason the IRS disallows deductions is lack of documentation.

831. They should know that using pirated software brings the FBI over for a chat. It's against the law.

•

832. They should know most large companies monitor Web surfing. Anything weird will bring the authorities.

•

833. They should know that sending chain letters by e-mail doesn't make them legal.

•

834. They should know how hanging out with the wrong people at the wrong time has helped introduce many people to the Feds.

•

835. They should know hacking into a company for fun and games can lead to black Suburbans parked in their front yard.

836. They should know the FBI can find out anything they want about anonymous e-mails, including registration information, session time stamps, and the originating IP address. Play nice.

•

837. They should know that if they even think about selling a controlled substance, the FBI will soon be interviewing their friends.

•

838. They should know to not let their sense of entitlement get in the way of their values.

•

839. They should know if they ignore their traffic tickets, the Feds won't come. But the sheriff will.

840. They should know the law sees
a huge difference between people who
buy club drugs and people who sell
them. People who buy them are merely
morons. People who sell them go to jail.

•

841. They should know stealing cable
signals breaks all kinds of laws. No
matter how easy it looks.

•

842. They should know that if they are
caught with drugs in other countries,
they'll wish the FBI had found them first.

•

843. They should know that if
they're thinking of doing something
even remotely illegal, they need
to check their self-esteem.

They Should Know God Loves Them Even When Nobody Else Does So a Spiritual Crisis Doesn't Cause Them to Move Home

844. They should know the most successful people rely on divine intervention.

•

845. They should know God
has anointed everyone with
special gifts. Even them.

•

846. They should know eternal truths exist.

•

847. They should know they'll
never learn anything by trusting
God only in the easy times.

•

848. They should know to consider
that maybe the world's problems
aren't its poor. But its rich.

849. They should know the poor are made in God's image as well as the rich. And He has written down specific instructions about the way they are to be treated.

•

850. They should know to allow divine grace to direct their lives.

•

851. They should know to decide in advance what kind of person they want to be in all situations. Or they'll leave themselves vulnerable.

•

852. They should know the best antidote to fear is realizing they're right with God.

853. They should know a powerful spiritual tool is to write letters to God.

•

854. They should know that extending forgiveness is the best way to be good to yourself after someone has been bad to you.

•

855. They should know that every time we say the Lord's Prayer, we ask God to forgive us as we forgive others. Yikes.

•

856. They should know to turn over each business meeting, each relationship, each dollar to His care. Each day.

857. They should know to not dwell on their mistakes. There was only one Perfect Human Being. Move on.

•

858. They should know to have an active prayer life before a crisis arises.

•

859. They should know that when people are highly stressed, they are most vulnerable to being recruited by a cult.

•

860. They should know God has a plan for them. And it is most likely different from their plan.

•

861. They should know to do something wonderful for somebody every day—and not get found out.

862. They should know everybody is dealing with something. Show grace.

•

863. They should know that people who make time for others seem to be guided by angels through life.

•

864. They should know that it doesn't matter their job title. They really only have one Boss.

•

865. They should know that doing the right thing, no matter how costly it seems at the time, always pays dividends.

866. They should learn to tithe 10 percent of their income to a church. The fact that it's not easy is the point. It's about trusting God that He will provide.

•

867. They should know getting knocked down is no excuse for losing their values.

•

868. They should know pride is the biggest roadblock to forgiveness. And leads to revenge.

•

869. They should know to be optimistic. Christ came to give us hope.

870. They should know that hope is a gift of the Holy Spirit. And when they feel like they're losing hope, to pray for it.

•

871. They should know that if they seek the best in all situations, they'll actually find it.

•

872. They should know the Holy Spirit will guide them to the people He wants them to meet and serve today.

•

873. They should know to not fear change. It's just evidence God is busy.

874. They should know that forty to fifty new religions are started every year. Any one could cause them to lose their way. Be grounded in what they believe.

•

875. They should know the purpose of the Bible is to know God and to make us holy.

•

876. They should know the funny thing about hope is that it takes a human to pass it on.

•

877. They should know to not pass up a chance to be useful in difficult situations. It's God calling.

878. They should remember
who really owns their body.
And to treat it accordingly.

•

879. They should remember
C. S. Lewis's statement, "If you aim
at heaven, you get earth thrown in;
if you aim at earth, you get neither."

•

880. They should know to read their
Bible before walking out the door.

•

881. They should know God
will never let them down.

They Should Know How to Avoid Getting Sued So They Don't Have to Spend All Their Money on Lawyers and Move Home

882. They should know it really helps to know an attorney before they need one.

•

883. They should know to not break any contract with their landlord, their health club, or their banker. Those guys sue.

•

884. They should know to never, ever sleep with anybody who works for them. Employees sue.

•

885. They should know to never loan their car to anybody. Someone gets in a wreck, someone sues, and kids move home.

886. They should know to get everything in writing. It's called proof.

•

887. They should know to pick up all the clutter lying on the floor before throwing a party. Strangers and drunks tend to sue when they trip and fall.

•

888. They should know to leave everything behind when they resign from a company except for personal files and items. Corporate documents, records, and files belong to the company. And they'll sue.

889. They should know to treat everyone with courtesy and respect. Even the drunk yelling at them in the bar at 2:00 a.m. They always have attorneys.

•

890. They should know to not post anything on the Internet or on a term paper that someone else created without getting permission. Writers sue.

•

891. They should know to not buy a pit bull. A lawsuit on four legs.

892. They should know to not let any drunk drive home from their apartment after a party. Big-time lawsuit.

•

893. They should know to not post compromising pictures of anyone. Embarrassed people sue.

•

894. They should know traffic accident victims can't wait to sue. Drive paranoid.

895. They should know to not crack sexual
jokes at work. Talk about gardening.

•

896. They should know to disable their
links to LimeWire, Grokster, Kaaza, and
other music-swapping services. The
music industry is suing everybody.

•

897. They should know to
negotiate extra fees and charges
found in apartment leases rather
than ignore them. Landlords sue.

898. They should know to get the ice off their sidewalk and porch. Nature can't be sued over someone falling, but homeowners can.

•

899. They should know lawyers will be calling if someone slips on wet floors, slippery stairs, or a messy floor. Keep everything picked up, show people the telephone cord stretched over the floor, and limit the alcohol intake.

900. They should know the danger of repeating rumors. Especially writing them down and getting them published. Angry people sue.

•

901. They should know that fighting can get them sued. Losers sue.

•

902. They should know to pay back their debts. Especially the ones they were hoping everyone would forget about. Like student loans. The government has battalions of lawyers.

903. They should know to not start a business while working for what could be a competitor. Ex-employers would rather sue than make a sale.

•

904. They should know to leave all the trade secrets of their employer at their employer. They'll lose the suit.

•

905. They should know spreading a sexually transmitted disease will result in lawyers calling. Sick people sue.

•

906. They should know they can be sued for delinquent child support. Man or woman.

907. They should know to negotiate late payments with doctors and hospitals before attorneys get involved.

•

908. They should know to pay attention to their surroundings. Is the elderly woman next to them holding a hot cup of coffee? She'll sue.

•

909. They should know who they're marrying. Jilted lovers sue.

910. They should know to save their paper-work and keep it organized. Save invoices, bills, statements, and tax returns.

•

911. They should know that often all it takes to avoid a lawsuit is producing a receipt.

•

912. They should know a cab is much cheaper than posting bond and dealing with a driving-while-intoxicated lawsuit.

•

913. They should know to keep copies of their really important documents some other place than their bedroom. Like a safe deposit box.

914. They should know about small
claims court. It's how the little guy can
sue the big guy. Without lawyers.

•

915. They should know legal
problems can't be solved later.
Deal with them now.

•

916. They should know divorce
is one long, expensive lawsuit.
And the kids always lose.

They Need to Know to Hold On to Their Ethics So They Don't Sell Out and Have to Move Home

917. They should know their ethics and values will always be under attack. It's the world we live in.

•

918. They should know to never be ashamed of doing the right thing.

•

919. They should know the failure of doing what is right will always haunt them.

•

920. They should know there is a difference between what is legally permissible and what is ethical.

•

921. They should always know where the "line" is.

922. They should know their reputation can shadow them all of their life.

•

923. They should know God cares about how they earn their money.

•

924. They should know God doesn't approve of anyone gaining profit by oppressing the poor. Even if 10 percent of the proceeds go to the church.

•

925. They should know confidentiality is a key to trusting relationships.

926. They should know to not accept praise and rewards they haven't earned. Send them in the right direction.

927. They should know the means don't justify the ends.

928. They should know to accept blame when appropriate, not pass it on.

929. They should know there's no such thing as an ethical dilemma. There's only a decision they don't want to make.

930. They should know it takes effort
to carry and nurse resentments.
Forgiveness soothes the soul.

•

931. They should know to live their lives
as an example. One day they'll have kids.

•

932. They should know that if they wait
to feel like doing the right thing, the
right thing may never get done.

•

933. They should know that if they do
anything that takes society down a
notch, they are lowering their ethics.

934. They should develop the inner strength it takes to stand up and say, "This is wrong." To their friends, to their company, even to their church.

·

935. They should know the consequences of unethical behavior are often jail, loneliness, debt, unemployment, and moving in with their parents when they're forty-five.

·

936. They should remember God is watching.

They Should Know How to Act and Think Like an Adult Because the Alternative Will Force Them to Move Home

937. They should know writing hot checks isn't just bad fiscal policy. It's against the law.

•

938. They should know that people with high self-esteem don't sleep around.

•

939. They should know that sex is a marriage sacrament, not a business transaction.

•

940. They should know betting with the rent money is high-stakes gambling. Drawing to an inside straight can bring them home.

•

941. They should know if they're continually depressed and feeling angry at those closest to them, it's time to quit drinking, quit partying, and go get some sleep.

942. They should know that if there's a history
of alcoholism or drug addiction in their family,
it's best they remain the designated driver.

•

943. They should know if their
behavior is secret or abusive,
it's only going to get worse.

•

944. They should know that people
who get so drunk they wind up in fights
are people who usually get carted off
to jail or the hospital. Or both.

•

945. They should know how to deal
with difficult people. Walk away
from a fight. Don't ignite it.

946. They should know that selling
their ADD medicine to anyone,
even a friend, is a criminal act.

•

947. They should know club drugs in bars
can lead to pregnancy, disease, and often-
times a trip to the emergency room.

•

948. They should know that behaving badly
at work doesn't build morale. It builds a case.

•

949. They should know their
desire for easy money is how a
con artist can pick them clean.

•

950. They should know that bad behavior is
not someone else's fault. It's a moral lapse.

951. They should know that if they're
screaming and yelling at people while
driving, their priorities have taken a left turn.

•

952. They should know it's better to face a
problem head-on. Not with a prescription.

•

953. They should know to watch their
language at work. Employee manuals
are written because of this.

•

954. They should know that if they are
difficult to get along with, they will have a
hard time keeping a job, keeping friends,
and keeping close relationships.

955. They should know calling someone over five times a day who doesn't return their calls makes them appear to be a stalker.

•

956. They should know being drunk or high is no excuse for bad behavior.

•

957. They should know if they're tempted to cheat on their spouse, they'll be tempted to cheat on the next one.

•

958. They should know to relax someplace besides in a bar.

•

959. They should know that if they're doing anything on the Internet at 3:00 a.m., they just might have a problem.

960. They should know employers and admissions officers at graduate schools are looking for candidates who demonstrate maturity.

•

961. They should know to pay their bills on time. Not just sit there and garner late charges.

•

962. They should know how to function in a world that couldn't care less whether they make it in life or not.

•

963. They should eradicate any sense of entitlement.

•

964. They should know to face problems as they happen. Not put them off until they're unmanageable.

965. They should not be afraid
to make a decision. And stick by it.

•

966. They should know that instead of
going to their parents for money, they
should work things out. Or do without.

•

967. They should know that a college degree
doesn't teach them everything, but it helps
prepare them to learn anything.

•

968. They should know that reading a
newspaper, belonging to a church, voting
for a president, and identifying with a
political party are all signs of adulthood.

969. They should know to never ever take out a home equity loan. If things don't go as planned, they're going to be looking for a new place to live.

•

970. They should know that no job, relationship, or situation ever goes according to expectations. Expect to be surprised.

•

971. They should know to use their time at college to network and make themselves marketable for at least two or three career possibilities.

•

972. They should know one of the worst things an adult can be labeled is immature.

973. They should recognize a substance abuse problem in their lives or in the life of those close to them. And get help.

•

974. They should understand that people who never have to work will never truly believe in themselves.

•

975. They should know supporting oneself financially and contributing to society are keys to maturity.

•

976. They should know stability doesn't involve changing career plans, lovers, and beliefs every six months.

977. They should know they could save a minimum of $15,000 by graduating in three years instead of four.

•

978. They should know to exercise self-control. In partying, spending, drinking, talking, and relationships.

•

979. They should know to not fear criticism. It's part of life.

•

980. They should know to go to every wedding they're invited to. It's a key to building and honoring lifelong relationships.

•

981. They should know to never miss a funeral of a friend or a friend's family.

982. They should know authority
figures are not the enemy.

•

983. They should know that a six-figure salary
comes with working your butt off in college,
then graduate school, and then in the workplace.

•

984. They should know constantly relocating
for school and work is a recipe for loneliness.

•

985. They should know that if they have tied
up more money in video games than books,
they might want to reevaluate things.

•

986. They should know what's important
and what isn't. A plasma TV isn't.
Graduate school is. It's called perspective.

987. They should know adults have to answer only to themselves. And God.

•

988. They should know college was the minor leagues. The white-collar world is a much more physically and mentally demanding environment.

•

989. They should put something on their iPod besides music. Sermons, lectures, and books are a start.

•

990. They should know to lower their expectations of other people, and raise them for themselves.

991. They should know that if they
focus on what's good today, they'll have
a good day. If they focus on what's bad,
the day will go down the toilet.

•

992. They should know to listen
to gain understanding, not
just enough to offer a flip reply.

•

993. They should know to not continually
interrupt, or people will think they're kooks.

•

994. They should know to pause before they
speak. A whole lot of stupid things will go unsaid.

•

995. They should know the ability to earn respect
is what separates the adults from the kids.

996. They should know that maturity is the ability to determine future consequences before making a decision.

•

997. They should realize failure can lead to maturity.

•

998. They should know to develop spiritual and mental endurance.

•

999. They should know God isn't finished shaping them.

•

1000. They should know they can make it without their parents.

•

1001. They should know to look forward. Not homeward.